# Catholic Positive Energy

By

George Goodsaid M.A.

# Table of Contents

# Foreword

Especially in our age of systems, experts, movements, and never-ending projects, it remains essential that Christian people approach others with simplicity. The Gospel is not first a program or an agenda—economic, social, or otherwise. It is, first and foremost, the radiant gift of God's love in Jesus Christ. To bring this love to others is the heart of evangelization: not to argue, not to impose, not to correct with severity, but to live—and to speak—outwardly as signs of the gift we have received within.

What is more, because we live in an age of systems, experts, movements, and never-ending projects, we can easily fall into the habit of treating others merely as difficulties. There is very little room for personalism in such a world.

What follows in these pages is testimony. And there is still a vital place for testimony. In fact, testimony will always be at the heart of the Christian way. When Andrew met Jesus, he did not compose a treatise or design a strategy. He went straight to his brother Peter and said simply, "We have found the Messiah." Having found Him, he turned without reservation and bore witness. This same spirit of witness breathes through the life and words of my friend George Goodsaid. His story is not one of perfection, but of a man who, despite hardship and pain, has chosen to let go of negativity and to make his own face and voice a testimony to Christ's goodness.

George has made a deliberate choice: to reject the poison of negativity, contempt, and bitterness, and instead to turn peacefully to the world. He has allowed his voice to become a voice for what builds up, rather than what tears down. This is not a shallow optimism, but a deep act of faith—an active will for the good of others even when hardship, pain, and rejection have touched his own story.

In an apparition to St. Joan de Valois, the Virgin Mary reportedly told her: "You shall seek to establish peace among all those among whom you dwell. You shall speak nothing but words of peace, concerned for the salvation of souls. You shall not listen to slanderous words, and as soon as you see some sinners, you shall say in your heart: These poor people must be saved." This, it seems to me, is the perfect advice for every modern, busy, anxious, and even angry Christian—all of us. George has gotten the memo!

An evangelist is one who has received a great gift and longs for others to receive it as well. That gift cannot be communicated through negativity, condemnation, or even mere moral correction. It can only be communicated by living outwardly as a sign of the grace received within.

George has allowed God to transform his past wounds into wellsprings of compassion. His witness is not theory but lived reality. His life proclaims the peace and goodness of Christ the Savior.

I loved reading his words here, not because they give us a perfect witness to a perfect life—we do not get perfect lives. What we get is the opportunity to choose. And George has chosen Catholic Positive Energy, his own term for shining the light of Christ on all things.

Cy Kellett, host

Catholic Answers Live

In a world characterized by negativity and criticism, George recounts his journey of overcoming childhood ridicule, harassment, and bullying. He discovered a fulfilling life through his faith in Jesus.

In his book, "Catholic Positive Energy," George shares his experiences of finding joy, peace, and forgiveness through meditation on Sacred Scripture and the Catechism of the Catholic Church. He recognizes his fundamental identity as a child of God.

George emphasizes the significance of treating others with honor and respect, enabling them to dignify themselves rather than resorting to criticism. He underscores the importance of living life to the fullest as a child of God.

"Dignification is better than criticism. Live life to the fullest."

*- Gilbert Alderete,*
*President Catholic Men's*
*Fellowship of California*

# A Personal Invitation from the Author

Dear Reader,

Thank you for opening your heart to *Catholic Positive Energy*. This book was written to share hope, healing, and the joy that comes from living in God's love. If the words you read here touch your spirit, I invite you to stay connected with me beyond these pages.

Join me on **Facebook** and **YouTube** at *Catholic Positive Energy*, where I share weekly reflections, prayers, and messages of faith to help us all live with more peace, positivity, and purpose. Together, we can continue spreading the light of Christ in a world that truly needs it.

Let's keep walking this journey of faith and positive energy, side by side, as children of God.

With blessings and gratitude,
**George Goodsaid**

# Chapter 1
# It all starts here

If you come from an upbringing that involves a lot of bad memories, trauma, or times when you did not feel love from loved ones, you are not alone. The purpose of this book is to help readers understand that no matter what kind of background you may have, you can find happiness, experience joy with our Lord Jesus Christ, and embrace positive energy in your life if you read what I'm about to share with you here. I am George Goodsaid, M.A., and this is *Catholic Positive Energy*. I understand the struggle regarding being around dysfunctional behavior. When I was a kid, I was yelled at, hit, and spanked more times than I care to remember. There were also some distant people who bullied me and humiliated me over insignificant, petty things. Also, when I was a kid, I was picked on and bullied every day for five years, and that became so horrific that I became homeschooled all through high school, and this was the best blessing I could have ever received. I found solace in the quiet of my home, away from the harshness of schoolyard taunts. As a child, I experienced life, relationships, and the love (or lack thereof) from family in ways I was too young to fully comprehend. Some of us are fortunate to have very caring and loving people who make us happy, and some of us are not as fortunate. I want to be clear that I am not a therapist, nor do I claim to have all the answers, but I do have life experiences that might resonate with you and, perhaps, offer some hope.

One memory that stands out to me was the desperate need I felt for attention. I remember trying everything: loud outbursts, hyperactive behavior, making every conversation about me, and wanting to be seen. I wanted people to notice me, to hear my pain, even if I didn't fully understand what that pain was. Thankfully, as I grew older, I learned to find my worth in God and no longer craved attention in the same way. Another thing I want to make clear is that I love my parents. They did the best they could with what they knew and had. This isn't a story of resentment; it's a story of healing and growth, and it's important that you understand that. Often, when I scroll through my feed on Facebook, I see a post from *The Power of Positivity*, which states, "I've never met a strong person with an easy past." It's a reminder that the strongest people aren't the ones who have lived perfect lives. Take a moment to think about that. Many people see someone with a smile, kindness in their heart, and a lot of positive energy and assume their life was flawless. This could not be further from the truth. Every human being, myself included, has faced struggles just like everyone else. The most positive people are often those who have endured the most hardship. I have a dear friend whose life story is filled with trauma, violence, and loss, yet today they are one of the most positive, radiant people I know. Today this friend of mine is the most positive miracle I have ever met in my life. Many times, God uses people who have difficult backstories to be positive instruments to help lead and evangelize all of God's children. Many people do not realize that, oftentimes, the most positive, enthusiastic, inspirational people in the world are also the ones who have experienced the hardest of times and the most painful traumas.

God uses people like *St. Augustine of Hippo*, who had a mistress and an illegitimate son before his conversion; *St. Paul* (formerly Saul), who used to be a persecutor of early Christians before his conversion on the road to Damascus (Acts 9:1–19); and our first Pope, St. Peter, who denied Jesus three times and then became our first Pope and an amazing leader at the beginning of the Catholic Church—which has existed for over 2,000 years—has been arguably one of the most positive, influential leaders in Church history, with a legacy that continues to influence the world. If these men could find redemption and become leaders of immense positive energy, so can we. Just because someone has a difficult past, has sinned, or has faced trauma does not mean they are beyond redemption or beyond doing great things for God and the world. Jesus Himself is the ultimate example of this. Think about the story of the *Good Samaritan* (Luke 10:25–37). A man, left beaten and broken on the side of the road, was ignored by the people who should have helped him. But the Samaritan, a person not expected to care, was the one who showed compassion. This story reminds us that healing and goodness often come from the most unexpected places. Like the Samaritan, you too can choose to be an instrument of healing in the lives of others, no matter your past.

The love of God is very powerful and exists in this world through God's faithful children who love him and others. Every human being has the potential to do positive things for the Lord and the world. *St. Philip Neri* has a very positive quote that says, "Never say, 'What great things the saints do!' but 'What great things God does in his saints.'" Our Lord Jesus Christ does wonderful things for each one of us, and it is also through the holy saints that we need to emulate if we are to spend eternity with our Father in Heaven. Another amazing quote that is filled with positive energy is from St. Teresa of Ávila. She says, "Let nothing disturb you; let nothing frighten you. All things are passing away; God never changes. Patience obtains all things; whoever has God lacks nothing. God alone suffices." I am sure that many of you reading this book can relate to some of the struggles I have shared. No matter how many emotional scars you have, I want you to know that they can be healed as long as you fully embrace our Lord Jesus Christ, and as long as you stay faithful to him and the Church he founded (Matt. 16:18).

Another very important thing you need to fully embrace is positive energy. What I mean by that is to always wake up and go to bed every day thanking God for another day and being alive; to always be happy regardless of what is going on around you; and to always cherish the fact that you are a child of God, that God will take care of you, and that you need to also cherish the people in your life who love and care for you unconditionally. There will be times in life when you feel alone, when you feel as though no one understands. I know this feeling well. But I also know that in those moments we must hold on to the truth that God sees us. He is always with us, even when we feel abandoned. You are not alone. I have walked this path of loneliness and pain, and I promise that you can make it through. Stay with me through this journey, and together we will embrace the healing power of God's love.

# Chapter 2
# We all need Positive Role Models

When I was a kid, I didn't have any positive role models. Sure, I had family members who loved me, but I was deeply unhappy because I was bullied relentlessly. It wasn't until I grew older and became a man that I realized, emotionally, my life was in turmoil. I carried so much unhealed pain, and it colored everything I did. On November 12, 2018, I was browsing Facebook and typed in the words: *positive energy*. What I discovered next changed my life in ways I could never have imagined. I stumbled upon a Facebook channel dedicated to positive energy, led by a woman who radiated the most infectious positivity I had ever encountered. She became a dear friend and played an integral role in my healing. Before I met her, I had never really used the phrase *positive energy* in my life. But this woman, with her joyful outlook and unwavering belief in the goodness of life, introduced me to a new way of being. She gave me a book she had written, and that book sparked the beginning of a life-changing journey toward healing and transformation. My emotional scars were deep, and the trauma I had experienced wasn't just going to vanish overnight. But with the friendship of this positive, joyful, and genuinely loving human being, everything began to shift. Her energy, her way of seeing the world, and her unwavering faith rubbed off on me, and for the first time in my life, I started feeling like a different person. It was her presence, her spirit, that started to heal the broken pieces of my heart. This is why I'm so passionate about sharing the message that no matter how awful the trauma or the negative things you've experienced in life, healing is possible. The key is to surround yourself with amazing people. There's an old saying: *You become like the people you spend the most time with.* My response to that is simple: if the people you're surrounding yourself with are guiding you in the best ways, then emulating their example is the best investment you can make in your life.

If we take a look at Sacred Scripture, the Bible, in *Proverbs 27:9*, it says, "Ointment and perfume rejoice the heart: so does the sweetness of a man's friend by hearty counsel." Our friends—those who truly care for us—are among the most valuable treasures we can have in life. The Scripture goes on to say in *Ecclesiastes 4:9–10*, "Two are better than one because they have a good reward for their toil. For if they fall, one will lift his fellow. But woe to him who is alone when he falls and has not another to lift him!" True friendship is a gift, one that is built on mutual respect, love, and positivity. In the *Gospel of John 15:13*, Jesus tells us, "Greater love has no one than this, that someone lay down his life for his friends." The power of a friend who loves you enough to lay down their life for you is immeasurable. If you have friends who are loyal, those who encourage you, those who would do anything to support you, cherish them. They are the ones who will lift you up in times of darkness.

One of the most profound lessons I learned on my journey was at a silent Men's Retreat in 2008. One of the priests there shared an acronym for "family": *Forget About Me, I Love You*. This truly resonated with me. When we think about family, it should be about selflessness, love, and support. *Proverbs 27:17* says, "Iron sharpens iron, and one man sharpens another." This means that as children of God, we are called to care for and support each other, not just in good times, but especially during our most challenging moments. When we connect with those who truly care, we become better versions of ourselves. Sadly, for most of my life, I wasn't treated well by a number of certain people I knew as a kid. They felt it was okay to bully me, disrespect me, and treat me poorly simply because I was younger than they were. And so, I made the difficult decision to distance myself from them. There are certain people whose actions are toxic to your growth, and it is okay to let them go. Over time, I've been blessed with some of the most amazing friends, people who treat me with love, respect, and genuine kindness. They have become my chosen family, and my true support system.

As I reflected on this, I recorded a broadcast on my YouTube channel, *Catholic Positive Energy*, titled I Have the Most Amazing Friends in the World. I shared how our Lord Jesus Christ created mankind with the intention for us to live in community. We are not meant to be isolated. Every human being is a child of God who deserves love and connection. The *Catechism of the Catholic Church* (paragraph #142) reminds us of God's invitation to us: "By His revelation, 'the invisible God, from the fullness of His love, addresses men as His friends, and moves among them, in order to invite and receive them into His own company.' The adequate response to this invitation is faith." God wants all of us to be happy, and He provides us with the people who will help us fulfill that happiness. *1 Thessalonians 5:11* urges us, "Therefore encourage one another and build one another up, just as you are doing." Our words are powerful. They have the ability to either build up or tear down. But the truth is, when we choose to lift others with our words, we ourselves are elevated in the process. There's an old saying: *Sticks and stones may break my bones, but words will never hurt me.* I don't believe that saying is true. Every time I see someone disrespecting or tearing down another person, I see the damage done. Even the strongest among us are wounded by harsh words. As a society, we need to be more mindful of how we speak to others. Our words have the power to heal or to harm, and we should always strive to be instruments of healing. Even the strongest police officers are hurt when they meet a difficult individual who is very negative and says hurtful things to them.

Jesus provides the ultimate model of love, care, and self-sacrifice when He refers to Himself as the *Good Shepherd* in *John 10:11–18*. He tells us, *"I am the good shepherd. The good shepherd lays down his life for the sheep."* This act of selflessness exemplifies the very core of what it means to be a positive role model, a person who puts others' needs before their own, even to the point of laying down their life. In this passage, Jesus reassures us that He knows each of us intimately: *"I know my own and my own know me" (John 10:14).* In a world that often feels isolated, this message is incredibly powerful. Jesus is telling us that we are not alone. He is always there, always guiding us, and always willing to lay down His life for our well-being.

As a positive role model, He shows us that leadership, strength, and true friendship are built on love, sacrifice, and care for others. We are called to emulate this example in our own lives. The most profound positive influence we can have on others is not through power or prestige, but through acts of love, kindness, and self-sacrifice. Jesus teaches us that in serving others with a pure heart, we fulfill our purpose as His followers. Healing, both emotional and spiritual, cannot happen in isolation. We were not made to walk through life alone. God created us for relationship, and it is through community—whether that be our friends, our family, or the broader body of Christ—that healing truly begins. Being part of a supportive, loving community provides a foundation where we can share our struggles and triumphs, where we can be uplifted and encouraged. It is in this environment that God's love can flow freely through us, healing our wounds and transforming our hearts.

*Ecclesiastes 4:12* reminds us, "A cord of three strands is not easily broken." When we build our lives around meaningful relationships, we strengthen ourselves and those around us. In my own life, the transformation I experienced was only possible because I had people who believed in me and supported me. I could not have healed alone. The joy I now experience is not solely my own—it is the result of the positive energy and love I have received from others. Just as Jesus demonstrated by being the *Good Shepherd*, we are all called to care for one another, to lay down our lives for each other in whatever way we can. We will certainly have fun in the next chapter.

# Chapter 3
# Why We Need to Lift People Up

We need to lift others up because God says so. As I previously mentioned in *1 Thessalonians 5:11*, *St. Paul* says, "Therefore encourage one another and build one another up, just as you are doing." This is more than just a suggestion; it is a divine command to bring positive energy, love, and encouragement into the world. Jesus also emphasizes this in the Gospel of Matthew, in Chapter 7, verse 12: *"Do unto others as you would want them to do unto you."*

Now, some may feel differently about this. You might ask, *"What if others don't treat me the way I treat them? What if they don't love me back?"* Believe me, I know how that feels. I've walked through the painful experience of unrequited love and mistreatment, as I shared in earlier chapters. But here's the truth: no matter how others treat us, it is not our job to let their negativity destroy the love and joy we carry inside us. That is their problem, and in the end, God will deal with them. Do not let anyone's cruelty steal your peace or diminish the love that is meant to shine through you.

We hear about the two greatest commandments in Matthew 22:37–39, where Jesus says, *"You shall love the Lord your God with all your heart, and with all your soul, and with all your mind. This is the great and first commandment. And a second is like it, you shall love your neighbor as yourself."* I am sure many of you reading this might be thinking, *"I don't have many people in my life who do these things for me. I don't feel loved or supported by the people around me."* I understand that feeling all too well. As I mentioned in the first chapter, my own childhood was filled with pain and rejection. But even in those moments, God was always with me. He provided me with positive role models, whether friends, mentors, or simply the grace of His love that helped me heal.

It is these positive influences that we must cling to, and that's where God's light shines brightest. Don't let rude people or those who don't care about you take up valuable space in your mind or heart. As the old saying goes, "In one ear and out the other." When others hurt us, we need to let it go, leaving the negativity behind. I promise, if you make Jesus Christ and your loved ones your main focus, you will find peace, joy, and a deep well of positive energy in your life.

Recently, at Holy Mass, my pastor, Father Frederick Costales, said something that stuck with me: *"Make sure you use your tongue for the greater good, because the things you say can either lift up or wound others."* The words we speak hold incredible power. They can either build others up or tear them down. Which legacy do you want to leave behind? Do you want to be remembered for the hurtful words you said, or for the love and encouragement you offered?

*Galatians 6:2* teaches us, "Bear one another's burdens, and so fulfill the law of Christ." To bear the burdens of others means we must look beyond our own struggles and be there for others in their times of need. It is not enough to be self-centered; we are called to care for each other, to lift one another up in love. It is through this selfless love that we fulfill Christ's law. In *Philippians 2:3–4, St. Paul* offers this profound advice: "Do nothing from selfishness or conceit, but in humility count others better than yourselves. Let each of you look not only to his own interests, but also to the interests of others." This means we are to be kind, to serve others selflessly, and to consider their needs as equally important, if not more so, than our own. When we live like this, we are not just reflecting Christ's love but actively participating in His mission of spreading peace and positive energy.

The words of Scripture often echo this call to positive energy. In *Hebrews 10:24–25*, God says, "And let us consider how to stir up one another to love and good works, not neglecting to meet together, as is the habit of some, but encouraging one another, and all the more as you see the day drawing near." This verse reinforces the importance of community and encouragement. It is in fellowship, in shared worship, and in mutual support that we find the strength to endure and the joy to thrive.

The Catholic Church is rich with teachings that encourage positive energy and love. In *Paragraph #2198* of the *Catechism of the Catholic Church*, it says, "This commandment is expressed in positive terms of duties to be fulfilled." This teaching reminds us that we are not only called to avoid sin but to actively do good, to uplift, support, and inspire others with our words and actions.

I have always disliked excessive *criticism*. When I was growing up, I was criticized a lot by teachers and others, and it hurt deeply. I never received praise or positive reinforcement. I also have a distant relative who still criticizes and finds fault with everyone in the family, and this is one of the reasons why most of us no longer speak to that individual. Criticism, especially when it is not constructive, can have a lasting impact on one's spirit. But, in contrast, positive reinforcement can heal and uplift, creating lasting bonds and fostering an environment of trust and love.

Have you ever noticed that when people around you speak negatively or criticize others, the entire atmosphere shifts? It becomes heavy, draining, and sad. Now, think about when people around you speak words of love, kindness, and encouragement. The atmosphere lightens, and positive energy fills the space. Imagine if the world made an effort to emulate the good works of Jesus Christ and the kindness of figures like *Mister Rogers*, whose life was a shining example of gentle, compassionate, positive energy and love. If we all sought to love and uplift those around us, the world would undoubtedly be a much more beautiful place.

We all need friends who love us unconditionally, and if we want to live our lives to the fullest, we must surround ourselves with those who encourage and inspire us to be the best versions of ourselves. I want you to think of the most positive person you know. If you can, try to keep that person close to you. Their positive energy will rub off on you, and you will begin to see the world through a brighter, more hopeful lens. It's a well-known fact that if we spend a lot of time with others, we begin to adopt their habits, behaviors, and attitudes. In this case, If we surround ourselves with positive people, we will naturally begin to reflect that positivity in our own lives. It is the best investment you can make in yourself. I've made it my goal to be a man of God, filled with positive energy, and to carry this light wherever I go.

In the Gospel of *John 10:11–18*, Jesus reveals Himself as the *Good Shepherd*, the one who cares for His flock with selflessness and love. He says, *"I am the good shepherd. The good shepherd lays down his life for the sheep."* This passage speaks to the depth of Jesus' love for us. He is not just a leader or a teacher; He is the protector, the guide, and the self-sacrificial friend who gives His life for ours.

In the context of lifting others up, Jesus exemplifies the ultimate positive role model. He gives His life for us, not out of obligation, but out of pure love. His example teaches us that true positive energy comes from caring for others, from being willing to sacrifice for their well-being. This kind of self-giving love is the essence of *Catholic Positive Energy*—spreading goodness by putting others first.

We were not made to live in isolation. Each and every one of us is called to live in community, to bear one another's burdens, and to share in each other's joys. God's design for us includes a vibrant network of relationships—family, friends, fellow believers—all of which provide support, encouragement, and healing. When we live in community, we can help each other heal and grow, reflecting the love of Christ in our actions.

# Chapter 4
# Moving on From the Past is Important

If there is one crucial lesson I've learned from my life experiences, it's that holding on to trauma from the past is never beneficial to us. I can recall several times in my life when I was still angry or hurt by something someone did to me years ago. At times, I held on to that pain and anger for years, not fully realizing how it was affecting me. Eventually, I learned the hard way that if someone has wronged us, and we haven't seen that person in a long time, holding on to those bad memories serves no legitimate purpose. My spiritual director, whom I also consider a dear friend, Father Mike Onwuemelie, C.S.Sp., once told me that when we hold on to past hurt, we are ultimately hurting ourselves. My best friend has told me repeatedly that if five years have passed, it's time to let go of the bad memories and resentment for the sake of healing and moving forward. Holding on to the past is like carrying a heavy weight on our shoulders that we were never meant to bear.

One of the most powerful examples of moving forward and embracing forgiveness is found in *John 21:15–19*, where Jesus forgives Peter after his denial. After Peter denied Jesus three times, he must have felt an immense weight of guilt and regret. However, in this passage, Jesus meets Peter on the shore after His resurrection, offering him a chance for redemption. Jesus asks Peter three times, *"Do you love me?" (John 21:15–17)*, and with each affirmation, He commissions Peter to "Feed my sheep." This powerful exchange shows that despite Peter's past failures, Jesus was offering him not only forgiveness but also a renewed purpose. Jesus' response is an invitation to move forward—not to be shackled by past mistakes, but to embrace a future filled with purpose and grace. God does not want us to dwell in our past mistakes but to rise above them, move forward, and fulfill the calling He has placed on our lives.

Another poignant story of forgiveness and letting go is the *Parable of the Prodigal Son (Luke 15:11–32)*. Jesus tells of a young man who asks his father for his inheritance, leaves home, and squanders it all in reckless living. When a famine strikes, he finds himself in desperate need, and he returns home repentant and broken. What happens next is a beautiful display of God's boundless mercy and forgiveness. The father, upon seeing his son from a distance, runs to him, embraces him, and says, *"For this my son was dead and is alive again; he was lost and is found"* (Luke 15:24). Despite the son's actions, the father does not dwell on his mistakes or hold a grudge. Instead, he forgives him completely and restores him to his place as his son. This story highlights the importance of letting go of past offenses. It teaches that forgiveness is not contingent upon the other person's worthiness but is a reflection of the love and mercy that God shows to each of us. The father's forgiveness symbolizes God's willingness to embrace us fully, no matter how far we may have strayed.

In our own lives, we can apply this lesson by forgiving ourselves and others. We must let go of the bitterness, anger, and resentment that can keep us stuck in the past. Instead, we are called to forgive, as God forgives us, and to trust in His grace to restore and heal all that was lost. A perfect example of this can be found in the TV show *Monk*, which I'm sure many of you are familiar with. Detective Adrian Monk, who lost his wife in a traumatic event, became so consumed by his pain that he held on to every negative experience he had ever suffered. There's one episode where he encounters someone who used to bully him as a child, someone who would dunk his head in the toilet and give him "swirlies." Monk held on to this pain for 30 years, and the people around him saw that it was unhealthy. His friends and colleagues encouraged him to let go and move on, but Monk couldn't see it. *Letting go*, as hard as it may seem, is vital to our emotional and spiritual well-being.

Ask yourself this very important question: *If someone has wronged you in the past and they are no longer a part of your life, is it really worth it to hold on to those memories?* These are the types of things every single person, every child of God, needs to realize in order to heal and move on with their lives. There are several Bible verses that emphasize the importance of moving on, and I want to share a few of them with you:

*Isaiah 43:18–19*: "Remember not the former things, nor consider the things of old. Behold, I am doing a new thing; now it springs forth, do you not perceive it?"

*Philippians 3:13–14*: "Brothers, I do not consider that I have made it my own. But one thing I do: forgetting what lies behind and straining forward to what lies ahead, I press on toward the goal for the prize of the upward call of God in Christ Jesus."

*Proverbs 4:25–26*: "Let your eyes look directly forward, and your gaze be straight before you. Ponder the path of your feet; then all your ways will be sure."

*Revelation 3:8*: "I know your works. Behold, I have set before you an open door, which no one is able to shut."

*2 Corinthians 5:17*: "Therefore, if anyone is in Christ, he is a new creation. The old has passed away; behold, the new has come."

*Hebrews 10:22*: "Let us draw near with a true heart in full assurance of faith, with our hearts sprinkled clean from an evil conscience and our bodies washed with pure water."

*Ephesians 4:26–27*: "In your anger do not sin: Do not let the sun go down while you are still angry, and do not give the devil a foothold."

Therapists, no doubt, meet people who are haunted by bad memories, and while I am not a therapist, I want to acknowledge the deep pain that many carry. But ultimately, it comes down to allowing oneself to heal and choosing to move forward. Every time I broadcast on my Facebook and YouTube channels, especially during the Meditation and Prayer sessions, I always emphasize: *"We are going to get rid of negative energy—just like throwing things in the trash, and we are not going to get it back."* When you throw things in the trash, do you ever think about retrieving them? Do you hold on to them and let them sit around your house? If your answer is no, then why is it that we don't do the same when it comes to personal traumas or problems with others? It's time to treat our pain the same way we treat the trash—throw it away and never go back for it. Yes, I understand it's easier said than done, especially when deep wounds are involved. But as we move through life, we find that healing is a journey, and it's one that God wants us to undertake.

It is impossible to be a positive person if we are holding on to negative memories from the past. It may take time, but eventually, with prayer, meditation, and God's guidance, we can learn to release the past and embrace the present. If you truly want to experience the positive energy and joy this world has to offer, you must make the decision to move on. Life is difficult, and I know that firsthand. Life is not always fair, but just because we are treated badly or unfairly doesn't mean that we can't find peace, happiness, or serenity. I believe with all my heart that every child of God can heal and find happiness if only we trust God to guide us through it. Through faith, we can be freed from the chains of the past. A helpful reflection in the *Catechism of the Catholic Church* (Paragraph #1490) explains, *"The movement of return to God, called conversion and repentance, entails sorrow for and abhorrence of sins committed, and the firm purpose of sinning no more in the future. Conversion touches the past and the future, and is nourished by hope in God's mercy."* This is the beauty of conversion and healing: we are not defined by our past mistakes or wounds, but by the mercy of God that transforms us into new creations.

Another lesson I've learned is that when I talk to people, especially those who don't know me very well, about the bad things that have happened to me, they rarely seem to want to hear it. Constantly talking about negative things can make others uncomfortable, and more importantly, it can prevent us from healing. The best place to share your pain is with those who know and care about you. Surround yourself with people who love you, not with those who will judge or ignore your suffering. I am the type of person who genuinely cares about others, even people I barely know, because that's what love is. God calls us to love all His children, and we should extend that love to everyone, even if they aren't family or close friends. As Jesus teaches us in Matthew 22:37–39: *"You shall love the Lord your God with all your heart, and with all your soul, and with all your mind. This is the great and first commandment. And a second is like it: You shall love your neighbor as yourself."*

When I talk about positive, uplifting things, I notice that those around me become happy. They feel the energy shift, and they want to continue to be around me. Positive energy spreads just as negative energy does. It's up to us to choose what kind of energy we want to radiate. The more positive we are, the more we inspire others to adopt that same attitude. The *Catechism of the Catholic Church* also offers this powerful reminder in *Paragraph #1880*: *"A society is a group of persons bound together organically by a principle of unity that goes beyond each one of them."* This unity is built on love and mutual support, and it's through this community that we find healing and strength. We are called to love and care for one another, creating an environment that nurtures growth and healing.

A priest named Father Mark Bertelli once told me, *"The past certainly defines who we are today, but it does not mean that we should live in the past."* We are not meant to live in our memories, whether painful or pleasant. We are meant to live in the present, fully embracing the opportunities and blessings that each day brings. As I always say before signing off on my broadcasts, *"You're a child of God. Dignification is better than criticism. Live life to the fullest."*

# Chapter 5
# Live Life to the Fullest

One of the most important catchphrases I live by is to live life to the fullest. I came up with this motto because, for many years, when I was very young, I did not truly live life to the fullest. I grew up in a family that struggled financially, and we weren't always able to do fun, expensive things like traveling the world. There were also countless moments in my life when I could have done more, but I chose to stay home, avoid new experiences, and shy away from trying new things—whether it was tasting new foods, visiting new places, or even stepping outside of my comfort zone. Living in isolation for so long, I eventually realized that I wasn't living a happy life.

As I grew older, I watched as others around me traveled the world, had fun experiences, and tried new adventures. I began to feel like I was missing out on fishing trips, cruises, and visiting new cities. When the pandemic finally subsided, I made the conscious decision to step out of my comfort zone. I tried new things like growing a mustache, eating haggis (which, by the way, was surprisingly delicious, even though I'm not Scottish), traveling to places like Sacramento and Reno, and attending WrestleMania. I am a huge wrestling fan. It was only when I began to embrace new experiences that I started to understand what living life to the fullest really meant. It's about stepping outside of the old habits, opening up to new possibilities, and finding happiness, serenity, and love by being thankful to our Lord Jesus Christ. It's about embracing the beauty of the Catholic Faith and the positive energy it brings into the world.

Jesus Himself says in *John 8:12*, *"I am the light of the world; he who follows me will not walk in darkness but will have the light of life."* These words remind us that following Jesus brings light into our lives, guiding us through the darkness and leading us to live fully. In addition to stepping out of our comfort zones and living fully in the present, Jesus calls us to live fully within His Kingdom. This is not just about seeking worldly pleasure but about embracing a life of faith, service, and growth through God's will.

One of the clearest examples of this call is found in the *Parable of the Talents (Matthew 25:14–30)*. In this parable, Jesus tells the story of a master who entrusts his servants with talents (a form of money) before going away on a journey. To one servant, he gives five talents; to another, two; and to the last, one talent. Upon his return, the master asks his servants to account for what they have done with what was entrusted to them. The first two servants doubled their talents, while the third servant, fearful of losing what he was given, buried his one talent. The master rewards the first two servants for their faithfulness and productivity, saying to them, *"Well done, good and faithful servant...enter into the joy of your master"* (Matthew 25:21). However, the third servant, who did nothing with his talent, is cast out.

This story illustrates how small acts of faith and diligent work in God's Kingdom can lead to abundant growth and eternal rewards. Living fully for God means using the gifts He has given us to their fullest potential, not holding back due to fear or uncertainty. Just as the servants were expected to act with faith and responsibility, we are called to live fully, trusting in God's provision.

Another beautiful example is the *Parable of the Mustard Seed (Matthew 13:31–32)*. In this parable, Jesus compares the Kingdom of Heaven to a mustard seed, which starts as the smallest of all seeds but grows into the largest of garden plants, offering shelter to the birds of the air. This simple story demonstrates how even the smallest acts of faith and the smallest beginnings in God's service can lead to great things. Just as a tiny seed can grow into something significant, a small step in faith can lead to a life that is fruitful and fulfilling in God's Kingdom. By embracing God's calling to live fully, we are choosing to take the small steps of faith—just as the mustard seed grows, so does our spiritual growth, one step at a time.

It's in these small acts of faith, done daily, that we begin to experience the fullness of life that Jesus promises. Living fully for God is not about grand gestures, but about the consistent, humble offering of ourselves to His will. In *John 12:36*, Jesus continues, *"While you have the light, believe in the light, that you may become sons of light."* Jesus calls us to follow Him and walk in the light, embracing a life filled with faith, hope, and love.

God's love for us is unconditional. He loves us even when we stray, even when we make mistakes. But this doesn't mean that we are free to act without regard for His commandments. In John 14:21, Jesus says, *"If you love me, you will keep my commandments, and he will be loved by my Father, and I will love him and manifest myself to him."* Love for God is shown in our actions by following His commandments and living out His will. We are called to be sincere in our faith, just as we are called to be sincere in our relationships with each other.

True love requires effort, trust, and obedience. In marriage, friendship, or our relationship with God, mutual commitment is key. Our salvation depends on our willingness to follow God and keep His commandments.

We, as children of God, should never settle into comfort zones because they create barriers. For instance, consider someone who is afraid to leave their home and decides to stay there, never exploring the world. By doing so, they miss out on experiences, adventures, and the beauty of other cultures. Living life to the fullest means breaking free from the barriers of comfort and seeking new, enriching experiences.

Even Jesus didn't have a comfort zone. He stepped into the wilderness, fasting and praying for 40 days in the desert. His life was a testament to being willing to face discomfort for the sake of a higher purpose. He set the ultimate example for us to follow. We are not called to seek comfort, but to seek happiness, positive energy, and holiness. As *St. Paul* reminds us in Philippians 4:4, *"Rejoice in the Lord always; again I will say, rejoice."*

True joy comes not from living in the comfort of routine, but from embracing the challenges and joys of living fully in God's light. It's about finding peace and happiness, even in the struggles, because we know that God is always with us. We are called to live life to the fullest, but how do we do that? We don't just live for the sake of enjoyment, but with purpose and gratitude toward God. Jesus wants us to be happy and filled with joy.

The Bible is full of verses that encourage happiness and positive energy:

*1 Thessalonians 5:16–18*: "Rejoice always, pray without ceasing, give thanks in all circumstances; for this is the will of God in Christ Jesus for you."

Psalm 16:11: "You make known to me the path of life; in your presence there is fullness of joy; at your right hand are pleasures forevermore."

*Matthew 5:4*: "Blessed are those who mourn, for they shall be comforted."

In each of these verses, we are reminded that true joy and fulfillment come when we live in alignment with God's will, trusting that He will lead us to a life filled with meaning and purpose. As we move through life, we must constantly ask ourselves: Would we be proud of the life we've lived if we were to look back on it at the end of our lives? Would we say we've lived life to the fullest, embraced each moment, and followed God's guidance? Or would we regret the time spent stuck in comfort zones or avoiding challenges?

The invitation Jesus offers is one of transformation, a call to live a life that is not only fulfilling but also holy. Being happy is not enough; we are called to be happy and holy. When we live according to God's will, we experience a fullness of life that transcends worldly achievements or possessions. We are called to embrace both joy and holiness, finding balance between enjoying the blessings of life and living with reverence toward God.

Lastly, I want to remind all of you wonderful people who took the time to read my book about the importance of the messages we've shared together. We need positive role models, people who lift us up, and we must surround ourselves with those who do the same. We need to move on from the past, throwing away past traumas like we throw away trash, and we need to live life to the fullest, embracing every opportunity for joy, growth, and spiritual fulfillment.

These are obstacles that many of us face—myself included—but with the right mindset and God's grace, we can overcome them and live the life He intended for us. If we all take these lessons to heart, we can find happiness, peace, serenity, and positive energy. I hope this book has been a positive and uplifting experience for you and that it has helped to enrich both your spiritual and personal life. Live life to the fullest, as a child of God, with dignity and love for others.

May God bless you abundantly, and please subscribe to *Catholic Positive Energy* on Facebook and YouTube.

www.ingramcontent.com/pod-product-compliance
Lightning Source LLC
Chambersburg PA
CBHW061720120626
46550CB00003B/1299